Written By

Kashan Ajmeri

I0410275

MASTERING ARTIFICIAL INTELLIGENCE A COMPREHENSIVE GUIDE TO AI TECHNOLOGY

10 CHAPTERS

LIMITED
★ ★ ★ ★ ★
EDITION

Mastering Artificial Intelligence
A Comprehensive Guide to AI Technology

INTRODUCTION: UNLEASHING THE POWER OF ARTIFICIAL INTELLIGENCE

In the grand tapestry of technological advancement, few threads have woven a narrative as profound and transformative as Artificial Intelligence (AI). In a world where innovation is the lifeblood of progress, AI stands at the forefront, poised to reshape industries, redefine human capabilities, and chart new horizons.

Imagine a world where machines not only mimic human intelligence but surpass it, where algorithms sift through mountains of data to unveil insights, and where everyday tasks are automated with unprecedented precision. This is the realm of AI, a domain where science fiction meets reality, and the possibilities are limited only by our imagination.

This eBook, "Mastering Artificial Intelligence: A Comprehensive Guide to AI Technology," is your passport to understanding and harnessing the vast potential of AI. Whether you're a seasoned technologist seeking to delve deeper into the intricacies of machine learning or a newcomer eager to grasp the fundamentals, this guide is designed to accommodate a wide spectrum of readers.

In the pages that follow, we embark on an exhilarating journey through the AI landscape. We'll decipher the inner workings of machine learning, explore the neural networks that underpin deep learning, and unravel the mysteries of Natural Language Processing (NLP) and Computer Vision. We'll also delve into the realm of Reinforcement Learning, where AI learns to make decisions through trial and error.

But this eBook is more than just a technical manual. We'll also confront the ethical quandaries that AI poses, addressing issues of bias, fairness, and transparency. We'll explore the real-world applications of AI across diverse industries, showcasing its transformative potential. And we'll peer into the future, where quantum computing and advanced AI promise to redefine our understanding of what's possible.

As we venture through the chapters, keep in mind that AI is not a distant concept; it's a dynamic, ever-evolving field with real-world implications. Whether you're a student, a professional, or an entrepreneur, understanding AI is no longer optional—it's essential for navigating the future.

So, fasten your seatbelts and prepare for an odyssey into the heart of AI. By the time you reach the final page, you'll not only comprehend the intricacies of AI but also appreciate its potential to revolutionize our world. Whether you're an innovator, a dreamer, or simply a curious mind, AI awaits, and this eBook is your gateway to unlocking its limitless possibilities.

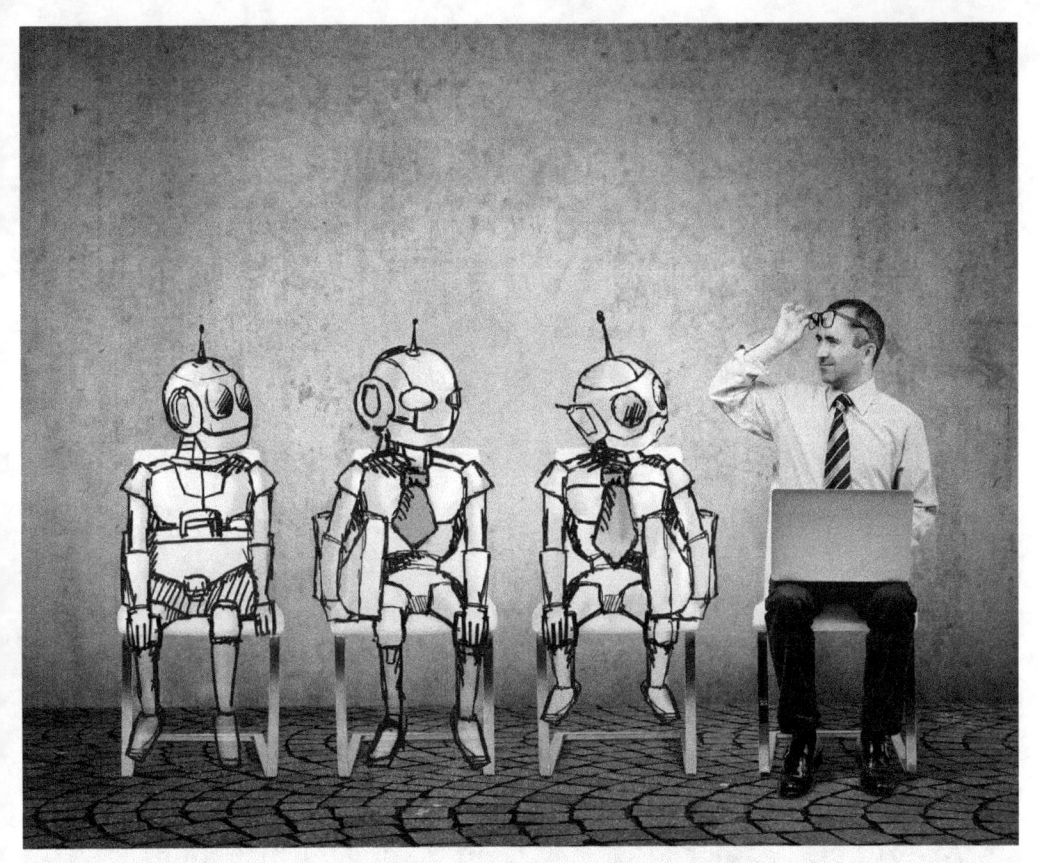

CHAPTER 1: UNDERSTANDING ARTIFICIAL INTELLIGENCE

Artificial Intelligence (AI) is a groundbreaking field of computer science that aims to develop machines capable of performing tasks that typically require human intelligence. AI systems can analyze data, recognize patterns, make decisions, and even interact with humans in natural language. This chapter serves as a foundational introduction to the world of AI.

1.2 Historical Perspective

AI's journey begins in the mid-20th century. Although the concept of AI dates back to ancient myths and legends, its formal inception came in the mid-20th century. We'll take a brief historical tour, highlighting key milestones:

- Dartmouth Workshop (1956): The birth of AI as a field.
- Early AI Programs: Developments like the Logic Theorist and General Problem Solver.
- AI Winter: Periods of reduced funding and enthusiasm.
- Revival: The resurgence of AI in the 21st century.

1.3 The Core Components of AI

Understanding AI's building blocks is essential. AI systems rely on several core components:

- Data: AI thrives on data. It requires extensive datasets to learn and make informed decisions.
- Algorithms: Mathematical and computational instructions that govern AI behavior.
- Computing Power: High-performance hardware accelerates AI computations.
- Expertise: Domain knowledge is crucial for developing effective AI solutions.

1.4 Types of AI

AI comes in various flavors, each with a different level of capability:

- Narrow or Weak AI: Designed for specific tasks, like image recognition or language translation.
- General or Strong AI: Possesses human-like intelligence and can handle diverse tasks.
- Artificial Superintelligence: A hypothetical AI that surpasses human intelligence.

1.5 The AI Learning Process

AI learns through experience. To understand how AI works, we need to grasp its learning process:

- Training Data: AI models learn from vast amounts of labeled data.
- Supervised Learning: The model learns from labeled examples.
- Unsupervised Learning: The model finds patterns and structures in data without labels.
- Reinforcement Learning: AI learns by interacting with an environment, receiving rewards or penalties.

1.6 Key Challenges in AI

AI is not without its challenges and limitations:

- Data Quality and Bias: Biased data can lead to biased AI systems.
- Ethical Concerns: AI decisions may raise ethical dilemmas.
- Explainability: Understanding and interpreting AI decisions can be complex.

1.7 AI in Popular Culture

AI's portrayal in popular culture has shaped public perception:

- Movies and Books: Iconic AI depictions in films like "2001: A Space Odyssey" and "Blade Runner."
- Media Hype: Media's influence on public understanding of AI.

CONCLUSION

Understanding the foundations of AI is the first step toward harnessing its potential. In this chapter, we've explored what AI is, its historical journey, core components, types, learning processes, challenges, and its place in popular culture. As we dive deeper into AI technology, remember that it's a dynamic field with incredible potential to impact various aspects of our lives. In the following chapters, we'll delve into specific AI technologies, applications, and ethical considerations that define the AI landscape.

CHAPTER 2: MACHINE LEARNING FUNDAMENTALS

2.1 Introduction to Machine Learning

Machine Learning (ML) is a subfield of Artificial Intelligence that empowers computers to learn from data and improve their performance over time without being explicitly programmed. This chapter serves as an in-depth introduction to the fundamentals of machine learning.

2.2 Core Concepts of Machine Learning

Understanding the foundational concepts is crucial to grasping the essence of machine learning:

- Data: Data is the lifeblood of machine learning. It includes input information and labels for supervised learning.
- Features: Features are attributes or characteristics of the data used for training machine learning models.
- Labels: Labels are the target values that the model aims to predict in supervised learning.
- Algorithms: Machine learning algorithms are mathematical procedures that learn patterns from data and make predictions.
- Model: A machine learning model is the representation of patterns learned from data, used for making predictions.
- Training: The process of teaching a model to learn patterns from data.
- Testing and Evaluation: Assessing the model's performance using testing data.
- Predictions: The model's output when it encounters new, unseen data.

2.3 Supervised Learning

In supervised learning, machines learn from labeled data. Key concepts and algorithms include:

- Classification: Predicting discrete categories or labels.
- Regression: Predicting continuous numeric values.

- Popular Algorithms: Discuss algorithms like Linear Regression, Decision Trees, and Support Vector Machines.
- Use Cases: Examples of supervised learning applications, such as spam detection and image classification.

2.4 Unsupervised Learning

Unsupervised learning deals with unlabeled data. Concepts and techniques include:
- Clustering: Grouping data points based on similarities.
- Dimensionality Reduction: Reducing the number of features while preserving important information.
- Popular Algorithms: Introduce algorithms like K-Means clustering and Principal Component Analysis (PCA).
- Use Cases: Discuss unsupervised learning applications, like customer segmentation and anomaly detection.

2.5 Reinforcement Learning

Reinforcement learning involves agents learning by interacting with an environment. Key elements include:
- Agent: The learning entity that interacts with the environment.
- Environment: The external system the agent interacts with.
- Rewards and Penalties: Feedback signals provided to the agent.

- Policy: The strategy the agent employs to make decisions.
- Popular Algorithms: Discuss reinforcement learning algorithms like Q-Learning and Deep Q-Networks (DQN).
- Use Cases: Real-world applications of reinforcement learning, such as autonomous robotics and game-playing AI.

- **2.6 Practical Machine Learning**

- Offer practical advice for those looking to work with machine learning:
- Data Preparation: The importance of clean, well-organized data.
- Feature Engineering: Techniques for selecting and creating relevant features.
- Model Selection: How to choose the right algorithm for a given problem.
- Hyperparameter Tuning: Optimizing model performance.
- Evaluation Metrics: Metrics like accuracy, precision, recall, and F1-score for model assessment.

CONCLUSION

Understanding machine learning fundamentals is a pivotal step in harnessing AI's power. In this chapter, we've explored the core concepts, types of machine learning, key algorithms, and practical considerations. Armed with this knowledge, you're well-equipped to delve deeper into the world of AI and machine learning, which we'll continue to explore in the subsequent chapters of this eBook.

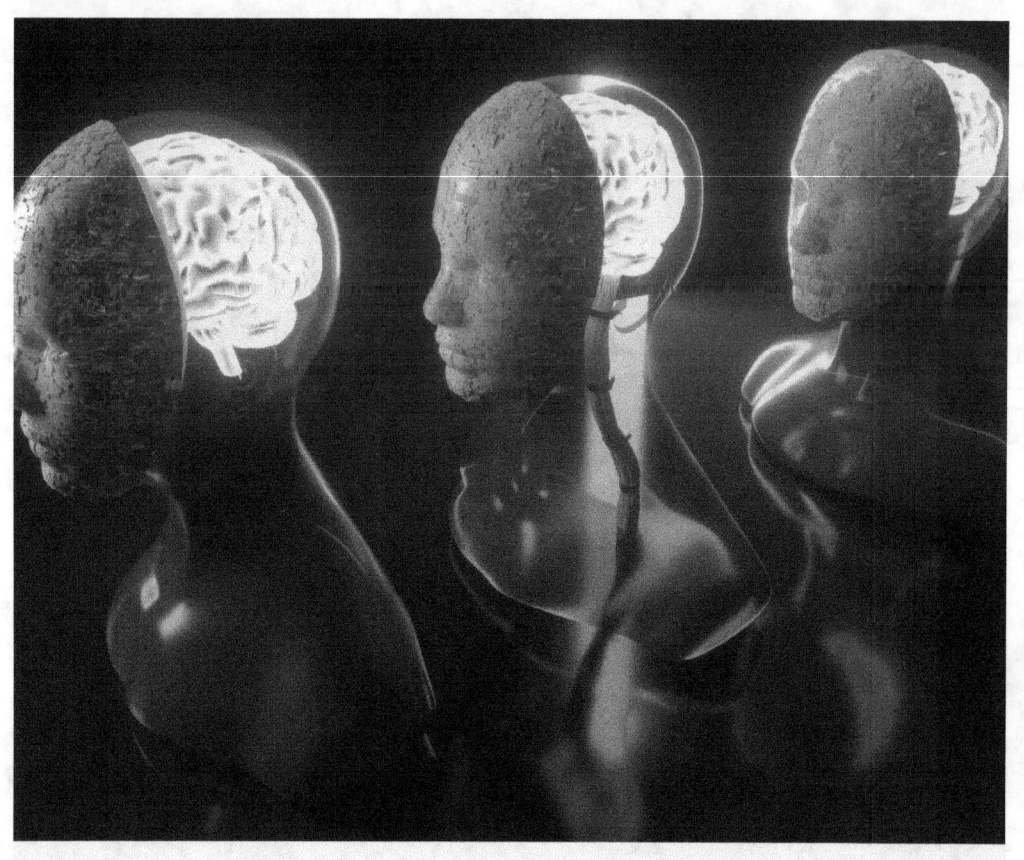

CHAPTER 3: DEEP LEARNING AND NEURAL NETWORKS

3.1 Introduction to Deep Learning

Deep Learning represents the cutting edge of machine learning, enabling AI systems to process vast amounts of data and make complex decisions. This chapter provides an in-depth exploration of the fundamentals of deep learning and neural networks.

3.2 Neural Networks: The Building Blocks of Deep Learning

- Neural networks are the foundation of deep learning. Key concepts include:
- Neurons: The basic processing units in a neural network.
- Layers: The arrangement of neurons into layers, including input, hidden, and output layers.
- Weights and Biases: How neural networks learn through weights and biases.
- Activation Functions: Functions that introduce non-linearity into neural network models.

3.3 Feedforward Neural Networks (FNNs)

- Feedforward Neural Networks are the simplest form of neural networks. Concepts include:
- Architecture: The structure of FNNs, including input, hidden, and output layers.
- Forward Pass: How FNNs process input data to make predictions.
- Training: The role of backpropagation and gradient descent in training FNNs.
- Use Cases: Real-world applications of FNNs, such as image classification and recommendation systems.

3.4 Convolutional Neural Networks (CNNs)

CNNs are specialized for processing grid-like data, such as images. Key elements include:
- Convolutional Layers: Layers designed for feature extraction.
- Pooling Layers: Reducing the spatial dimensions of data.
- Fully Connected Layers: Making predictions based on extracted features.
- Use Cases: Applications of CNNs in image recognition, object detection, and image segmentation.

3.5 Recurrent Neural Networks (RNNs)

RNNs are designed for sequential data, like text or time-series data. Concepts include:
- Recurrent Layers: How RNNs maintain a hidden state to process sequences.
- Long Short-Term Memory (LSTM): A specialized RNN architecture for handling long-term dependencies.
- Applications: Discuss use cases such as natural language processing, speech recognition, and time-series prediction.

3.6 Deep Learning Frameworks
Deep learning frameworks provide tools for building and training neural networks. Examples include TensorFlow, PyTorch, and Keras. Discuss the importance of these frameworks in simplifying deep learning model development.

3.7 Ethical Considerations in Deep Learning

Examine the ethical challenges associated with deep learning, including issues related to bias, fairness, transparency, and privacy. Discuss strategies for addressing these concerns.

3.8 Future of Deep Learning

Explore the future of deep learning, including emerging technologies, research directions, and potential applications. Discuss the integration of deep learning with other AI disciplines.

Conclusion

Deep learning and neural networks are at the forefront of AI innovation. In this chapter, we've dived deep into the principles and architectures that underpin deep learning, from feedforward networks to convolutional and recurrent networks. As we move forward in this eBook, we'll continue to explore the applications and evolving landscape of AI and deep learning, making it easier for you to harness the transformative power of these technologies.

CHAPTER 4: NATURAL LANGUAGE PROCESSING (NLP)

4.1 Introduction to Natural Language Processing

Natural Language Processing (NLP) is a branch of artificial intelligence that focuses on the interaction between computers and human language. It enables machines to understand, interpret, and generate human language, opening the door to a wide range of applications. In this chapter, we will delve into the fascinating world of NLP.

4.2 The Challenges of Language Understanding

Understanding human language is a complex task due to its inherent ambiguity and context-dependent nature. Explore the challenges NLP faces, such as:

- Ambiguity: Words and phrases with multiple meanings.
- Syntax: Understanding sentence structure and grammar.
- Semantics: Extracting meaning from words and phrases.
- Context: Grasping the significance of words in context.

4.3 NLP Techniques and Tools

Explore the fundamental techniques and tools used in NLP:

- Tokenization: Breaking text into words or phrases (tokens).
- Part-of-Speech Tagging (POS): Labeling words with their grammatical categories.
- Named Entity Recognition (NER): Identifying entities like names, dates, and locations in text.
- Parsing: Analyzing sentence structure.
- Word Embeddings: Representing words as dense vectors for machine learning.

4.4 Sentiment Analysis

Sentiment analysis is a common NLP application that assesses the sentiment or emotional tone of text. Discuss:

- Positive, Negative, Neutral: Classifying sentiment into categories.

- Use Cases: Sentiment analysis applications in social media, product reviews, and customer feedback.
- Challenges: Handling sarcasm, irony, and context-specific sentiment.

4.5 Text Classification

Text classification involves assigning labels or categories to text documents. Explore:
- Supervised Learning: Using labeled data to train text classifiers.
- Use Cases: Document categorization, spam detection, and news article classification.
- Popular Algorithms: Introduce algorithms like Naive Bayes and Support Vector Machines for text classification.
-

4.6 Machine Translation

Machine translation is the process of automatically translating text from one language to another. Discuss:
- Challenges: Language nuances, idiomatic expressions, and context.
- Neural Machine Translation (NMT): The evolution of machine translation using neural networks.
- Use Cases: Applications like Google Translate and language localization.

4.7 Conversational AI and Chatbots

Examine the role of NLP in creating conversational AI systems and chatbots:
- Dialog Systems: How chatbots generate human-like responses.
- Use Cases: Customer support, virtual assistants, and automated messaging.

4.8 Ethics and Bias in NLP

- Discuss the ethical considerations in NLP, including:
- Bias in Data: How biased training data can result in biased AI systems.
- Fairness: The importance of creating unbiased and fair NLP models.
- Transparency: Making NLP models more interpretable and explainable.
-

4.9 Future Trends in NLP

- Explore the future of NLP, including:
- Multilingual NLP: Advancements in handling multiple languages.
- Transformative Models: Discuss cutting-edge models like GPT-4 and BERT.
- AI in Content Creation: The role of NLP in generating human-like text and content.

Conclusion

NLP is a captivating field at the intersection of linguistics and artificial intelligence. In this chapter, we've explored its foundations, techniques, applications, and ethical considerations. As we continue our journey through the world of AI, NLP will prove to be an essential tool for understanding and interacting with human language, making it a pivotal aspect of modern technology and communication.

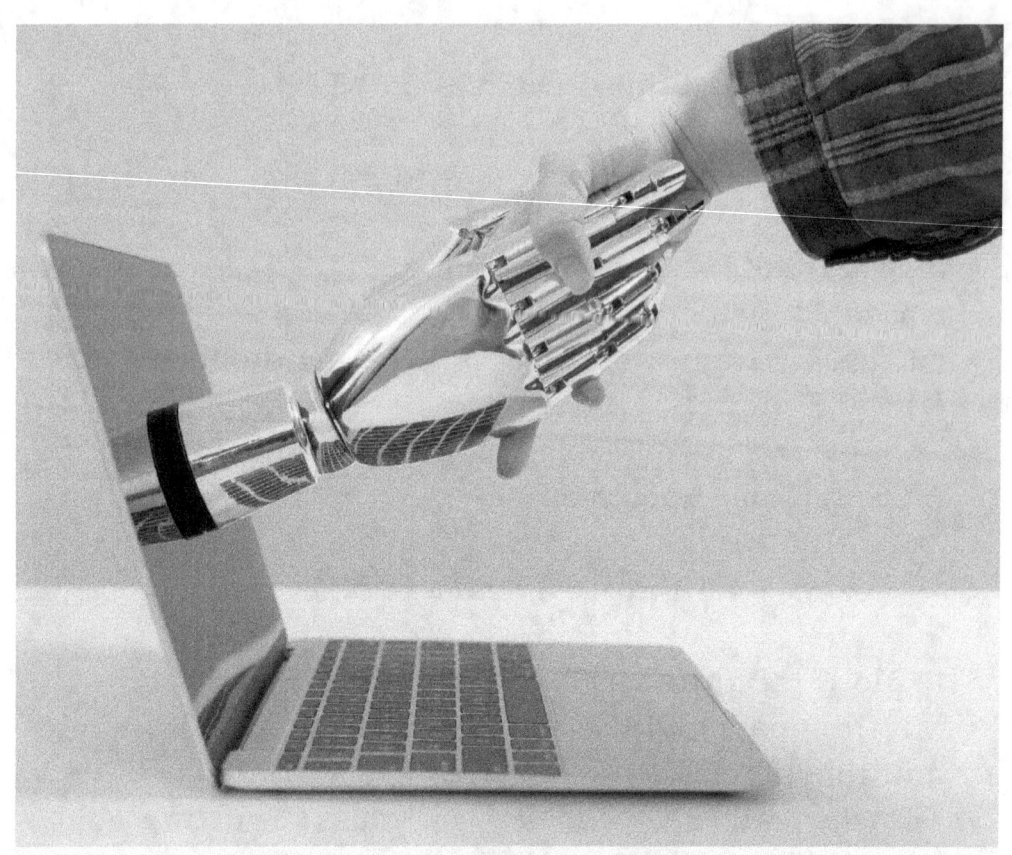

CHAPTER 5: COMPUTER VISION)

Introduction to Computer Vision

Computer Vision is a field of artificial intelligence that empowers machines to interpret and understand the visual world. It enables computers to analyze and make sense of images and videos, mimicking the human ability to perceive and interpret visual information. In this chapter, we will embark on a journey into the realm of Computer Vision.

5.2 The Complexity of Visual Data

Visual data is rich and complex, making computer vision a challenging field. Explore the complexities involved:

- Image Formation: How images are captured and represented digitally.
- Variability: Differences in lighting, perspective, and appearance.
- Object Recognition: Identifying and categorizing objects within images.
- Scene Understanding: Grasping the context and relationships in a scene.

5.3 Key Concepts in Computer Vision

Uncover the core concepts and techniques used in Computer Vision:

- Image Preprocessing: Techniques for enhancing and preparing images for analysis.
- Feature Extraction: Identifying distinctive patterns or features in images.
- Object Detection: Locating and recognizing objects within an image.
- Image Segmentation: Dividing an image into meaningful regions.
- Deep Learning for Computer Vision: The role of neural networks in image analysis.

5.4 Image Classification

Image classification is a fundamental task in Computer Vision. Discuss:

- Supervised Learning: Training models to classify images into predefined categories.
- Convolutional Neural Networks (CNNs): The architecture that revolutionized image classification.
- Applications: Examples of image classification tasks, including species identification and disease diagnosis.

5.5 Object Detection and Localization

Object detection goes beyond classification by identifying and locating objects within an image:

- Bounding Boxes: Defining regions around detected objects.
- Region-based CNNs: Techniques like Faster R-CNN for object detection.
- Use Cases: Real-world applications such as autonomous vehicles and facial recognition.

5.6 Image Segmentation

Image segmentation divides an image into meaningful segments or regions:

- Semantic Segmentation: Labeling each pixel with a class (e.g., road, car, sky).
- Instance Segmentation: Distinguishing between individual instances of the same class.
- Use Cases: Applications in medical imaging and autonomous robotics.

5.7 3D Computer Vision

Explore the extension of Computer Vision into the three-dimensional world:

Stereo Vision: Using multiple cameras to capture depth information.
3D Reconstruction: Building 3D models from 2D images.
Applications: Robotics, augmented reality, and virtual reality.

5.8 Ethical Considerations in Computer Vision

Examine the ethical implications of Computer Vision, including issues related to privacy, surveillance, and bias in image recognition.

5.9 Future Trends in Computer Vision

Discover the future of Computer Vision:

Multimodal Vision: Combining visual data with other sensory inputs.
Human-Machine Collaboration: The role of Computer Vision in human-robot interaction.
Advanced Object Detection: Improvements in real-time object detection and tracking.

Conclusion

Computer Vision is reshaping industries, from healthcare and automotive to entertainment and security. In this chapter, we've explored its foundations, techniques, and applications, highlighting its potential to revolutionize the way we perceive and interact with the visual world. As we venture deeper into the AI landscape, Computer Vision will continue to play a pivotal role in enhancing technology and expanding our understanding of the visual realm.

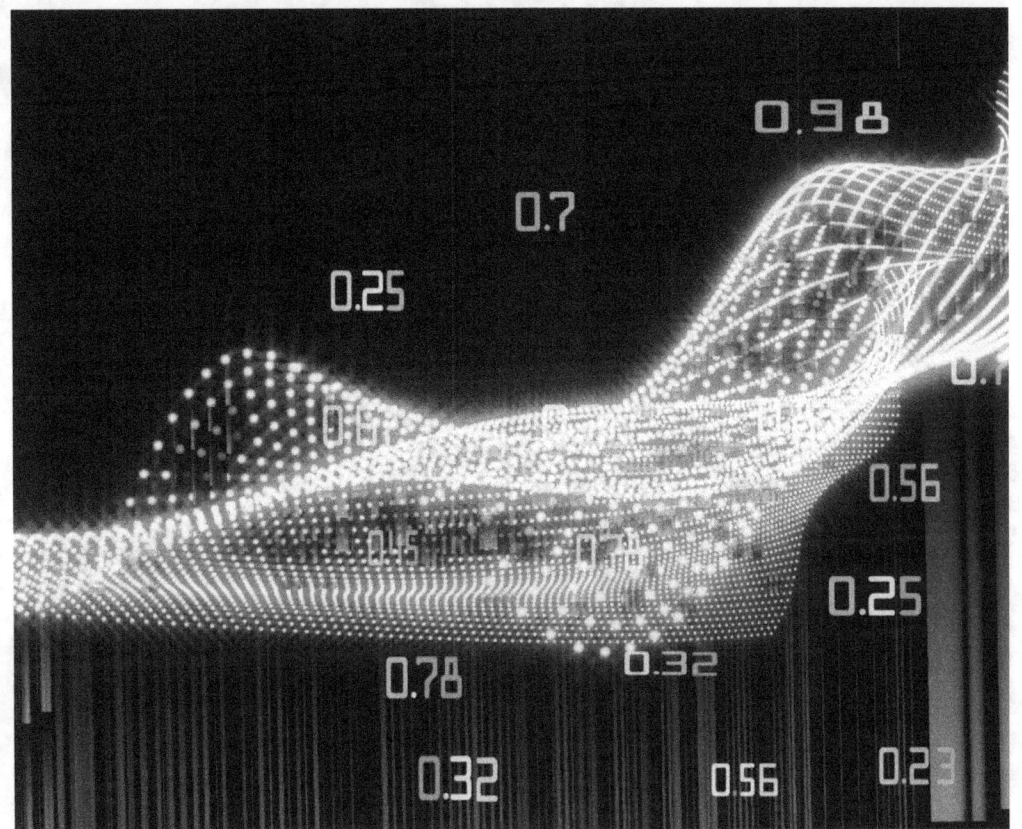

CHAPTER 6: REINFORCEMENT LEARNING)

Introduction to Reinforcement Learning

Reinforcement Learning (RL) is a machine learning paradigm in which an agent learns to make sequences of decisions in an environment to achieve a specific goal. It learns through trial and error, receiving feedback in the form of rewards or punishments based on its actions, with the aim of optimizing its decision-making policy to maximize long-term rewards. RL is often used in scenarios where actions affect future states and outcomes, such as in robotics, game playing, and autonomous systems.

Reinforcement Learning (RL): A Comprehensive Overview

Reinforcement Learning (RL) is a dynamic and exciting subfield of machine learning that has gained significant attention in recent years due to its potential to tackle complex decision-making problems. RL is a type of machine learning where an intelligent agent learns to make a sequence of decisions in an environment to achieve a particular goal. This goal can vary widely, from mastering video games to controlling autonomous vehicles, managing financial portfolios, and even optimizing healthcare treatments.

At the heart of RL lies the idea of learning through interaction. Unlike traditional supervised learning, where the model is trained on labeled data with predefined correct answers, RL agents learn by interacting with an environment, taking actions, and observing the consequences of those actions. This interaction is fundamental to RL and closely mirrors how humans and animals learn from their experiences.

The Core Components of Reinforcement Learning

To understand RL comprehensively, it's crucial to grasp its core components:

1. Agent: The learner or decision-maker that interacts with the environment. This can be a software agent controlling a robot, a trading algorithm, or even a human player in a video game.
2. Environment: The external system with which the agent interacts. The environment is dynamic and responds to the agent's actions. It could be a physical world, a simulation, a virtual game environment, or any context where decisions need to be made.
3. State (s): A representation of the current situation or configuration of the environment. States encapsulate all relevant information the agent needs to make decisions. For instance, in a game of chess, the state includes the positions of all the pieces.
4. Action (a): The set of possible moves or decisions the agent can make in a given state. Actions can be discrete (e.g., moving left or right) or continuous (e.g., adjusting the throttle of a vehicle).
5. Policy (π): The strategy or function that defines the agent's behavior. It specifies which action to take in a given state. The policy can be deterministic (always choosing the same action in a given state) or stochastic (choosing actions with probabilities).
6. **Reward (r)**: A numerical signal provided by the environment to evaluate the quality of the agent's actions. The reward indicates the immediate benefit or cost associated with an action taken by the agent. It serves as the feedback mechanism guiding the agent's learning.
7. **Value Function (V)**: A function that estimates the expected cumulative reward an agent can achieve from a given state while following a particular policy. It quantifies the long-term desirability of states under the policy.
8. **Model (optional)**: A model of the environment that predicts the consequences of actions. Models can be used for simulation and planning, aiding the agent in making decisions.

The RL Learning Process

Reinforcement Learning is a continuous, iterative learning process that unfolds over time:

- Initialization: The agent starts with little to no knowledge of the environment or the best actions to take.
- Exploration vs. Exploitation: The agent balances exploring new actions to discover better strategies and exploiting known strategies to maximize immediate rewards.
- Action Selection: The agent selects actions based on its policy, which can be either predefined or learned from experience.
- Interaction: The agent takes actions in the environment, transitioning from one state to another and receiving rewards based on its actions.
- Learning: The agent updates its policy and value estimates based on the rewards received and experiences gained. This process involves trial-and-error learning.
- Iterate: Steps 3 to 5 are repeated iteratively as the agent refines its policy and value estimates over time.
- Convergence: Over time, the agent aims to converge towards an optimal policy that maximizes its expected cumulative reward.

Exploring RL Algorithms

To achieve the learning process described above, RL utilizes various algorithms and approaches, including:

- Value Iteration: An approach that iteratively estimates the value function and uses it to find the optimal policy.
- Policy Iteration: An alternative approach that iteratively refines the policy and value function until an optimal policy is found.

- Monte Carlo Methods: Techniques that estimate value functions and policies through random sampling of episodes (sequences of actions and states) in the environment.
- Temporal Difference (TD) Learning: Methods that combine elements of both Monte Carlo and dynamic programming approaches, estimating value functions and policies based on experienced transitions.
- Q-Learning: A popular off-policy RL algorithm that learns the optimal action-value function, known as the Q-function.
- Deep Reinforcement Learning: Combining RL with deep neural networks to handle high-dimensional input spaces, this approach has been particularly successful in solving complex tasks, leading to breakthroughs like AlphaGo and self-driving cars.

Applications of Reinforcement Learning

Reinforcement Learning has demonstrated its versatility and potential in a wide range of applications:

- Game Playing: RL has excelled in mastering games like chess, Go, and video games, often surpassing human performance.
- Robotics: RL is used in robotics to enable robots to learn how to perform tasks in the real world, from walking to complex manipulation tasks.
- Autonomous Systems: Autonomous vehicles and drones utilize RL to navigate and make real-time decisions in dynamic environments.
- Finance: RL is applied to algorithmic trading, portfolio optimization, and risk management.
- Healthcare: RL plays a role in optimizing treatment plans, drug discovery, and personalized medicine.
- Natural Language Processing (NLP): RL aids in dialog system development, chatbots, and language understanding.
- Recommendation Systems: Content recommendation systems, like those used by streaming services, employ RL to suggest personalized content.
- Energy Management: Optimizing energy consumption in smart grids and buildings.

Challenges and Future Directions

While RL has made remarkable progress, it still faces several challenges:

1. Sample Efficiency: RL often requires a substantial amount of data and experience to learn effectively, making it less efficient compared to some other machine learning approaches.
2. Exploration Strategies: Balancing exploration and exploitation remains a challenging problem, particularly in high-stakes environments.
3. Safety and Ethics: Ensuring that RL agents make ethical and safe decisions is a growing concern.
4. Generalization: Enhancing an agent's ability to generalize knowledge from one context to another is a research priority.
5. Real-world Applications: Adapting RL to real-world applications with noise, uncertainty, and complex dynamics remains a significant challenge.

Despite these challenges, RL continues to evolve and promises to revolutionize various domains. Researchers are actively working on addressing these issues, and the field continues to make significant strides towards more intelligent, adaptive, and capable agents.

In conclusion, Reinforcement Learning is a dynamic and exciting area of machine learning that empowers agents to make intelligent decisions through interaction with their environments. With its broad range of applications and ongoing advancements, RL has the potential to reshape industries and improve our ability to solve complex problems in the real world. As the field progresses, we can look forward to more sophisticated RL algorithms and applications that enhance automation, decision-making, and our understanding of intelligent agents.

CHAPTER 7: AI ETHICS AND BIAS

Introduction to AI Ethics and Bias

AI ethics and bias are two critical and interconnected topics in the field of artificial intelligence (AI). Let's explore each of these concepts in more detail:

AI Ethics: AI ethics refers to the moral principles and guidelines that should govern the development and use of artificial intelligence systems. The goal of AI ethics is to ensure that AI technologies are developed and deployed in ways that are fair, just, and beneficial to society. Some key principles and considerations in AI ethics include:

Fairness: Ensuring that AI systems do not discriminate against individuals or groups based on factors such as race, gender, age, or socioeconomic status. This includes addressing both blatant and subtle forms of bias in AI algorithms.

Transparency: Making AI systems more understandable and interpretable to users and stakeholders. Transparency involves providing clear explanations of how AI decisions are made and the data and algorithms used.

Accountability: Holding individuals and organizations responsible for the actions and decisions of AI systems. This includes establishing clear lines of responsibility and mechanisms for redress in case of harm.

Privacy: Protecting the privacy and personal data of individuals when collecting, storing, and processing data for AI applications.

Safety: Ensuring that AI systems are designed and tested to minimize the risk of harm to people and property.

Beneficence: Focusing on the positive impact of AI on society and striving to maximize benefits while minimizing harm.

Beneficence: Focusing on the positive impact of AI on society and striving to maximize benefits while minimizing harm.

Bias in AI

Bias in AI refers to the presence of unfair and discriminatory behavior in AI systems, often resulting from biased training data or biased algorithm design. AI bias can manifest in various ways, including:

Data Bias: When training data used to develop AI models is not representative of the real world, it can lead to biased outcomes. For example, if a facial recognition system is primarily trained on data from one demographic group, it may perform poorly on other groups.

Algorithmic Bias: Biases can be introduced into AI algorithms during the design and development process. These biases may reflect the values or perspectives of the developers and can result in discriminatory outcomes.

Feedback Loop Bias: AI systems can reinforce existing biases in society. For example, if a recommendation algorithm suggests content that aligns with a user's existing beliefs, it can create feedback loops that reinforce those beliefs and limit exposure to diverse perspectives.

Addressing bias in AI is a key ethical concern. It involves:

Data Collection and Preprocessing: Ensuring that training data is diverse, representative, and free from biases. Data preprocessing techniques can be used to mitigate existing biases in data.

Algorithm Design: Developing algorithms that are designed to minimize bias and discrimination. Techniques like fairness-aware machine learning can help in this regard.

Continuous Monitoring and Auditing: Regularly evaluating AI systems for bias and taking corrective actions when biases are identified.

Diverse and Ethical Development Teams: Ensuring that AI development teams are diverse and inclusive, as diverse perspectives can help identify and mitigate bias.

AI ethics and bias are ongoing concerns as AI technologies continue to evolve and play increasingly important roles in our lives. It is essential for researchers, developers, policymakers, and society as a whole to work together to ensure that AI benefits everyone and does not perpetuate or amplify existing inequalities and biases.

CHAPTER 8: AI IN INDUSTRY

Introduction to AI in Industry

Artificial Intelligence (AI) has made significant inroads into various industries, transforming the way businesses operate, make decisions, and provide services. Here are some key ways AI is being used in various industries:

HEALTHCARE

Diagnosis and Treatment: AI-powered systems can assist doctors in diagnosing diseases, analyzing medical images (like X-rays and MRIs), and recommending personalized treatment plans.

Drug Discovery: AI accelerates drug discovery by analyzing vast datasets to identify potential drug candidates and predict their efficacy.

FINANCE

Algorithmic Trading: AI algorithms can analyze market data and execute trades at high speeds, making financial markets more efficient.

Risk Assessment: AI models are used to assess credit risk, fraud detection, and investment portfolio optimization.

Customer Service: Chatbots and virtual assistants help with customer inquiries, account management, and financial advice.

MANUFACTURING

Predictive Maintenance: AI analyzes sensor data to predict equipment failures, reducing downtime and maintenance costs.

Quality Control: Computer vision AI systems inspect products for defects in real-time on production lines.

Supply Chain Optimization: AI optimizes logistics, inventory management, and demand forecasting.

RETAIL

Recommendation Systems: AI algorithms analyze customer behavior to provide personalized product recommendations.

Inventory Management: AI optimizes inventory levels and reduces waste by predicting demand patterns.

Visual Search: AI enables visual search in e-commerce, allowing customers to find products using images.

AUTOMOTIVE

Autonomous Vehicles: AI powers self-driving cars by processing sensor data to to make real-time driving decisions.

Advanced Driver Assistance Systems (ADAS): AI enhances safety through features like lane-keeping, adaptive cruise control, and collision avoidance.

AGRICULTURE

Precision Farming: AI analyzes data from drones, satellites, and sensors to optimize crop planting, irrigation, and harvesting.
Crop Disease Detection: Computer vision helps identify and treat crop diseases early.

ENERGY

Smart Grids: AI manages and optimizes the distribution of electricity in smart grids, reducing energy waste and costs.
Predictive Maintenance for Utilities: AI predicts equipment failures in power plants and utility infrastructure.

EDUCATION

Personalized Learning: AI adapts educational content to individual student needs, improving learning outcomes.

Automated Grading: AI systems can automatically grade assignments and tests, saving educators time.

ENTERTAINMENT

Content Recommendation: Streaming services use AI to recommend movies, shows, and music based on user preferences.

Content Creation: AI can generate art, music, and even write news articles and scripts.

AEROSPACE

Flight Simulation: AI is used in flight simulators for pilot training and testing.

Aircraft Maintenance: Predictive maintenance systems help airlines optimize aircraft maintenance schedules.

AI's impact on industries is continually evolving as technology advances and businesses find new applications for AI-driven solutions. However, ethical and regulatory considerations, as well as addressing potential biases and security concerns, are crucial aspects of AI adoption across all sectors.

CHAPTER 9: THE FUTURE OF AI

Introduction to The Future of AI

The future of artificial intelligence (AI) holds tremendous potential and is likely to shape various aspects of our lives in profound ways. Here are some key trends and developments expected in the future of AI:

Advanced Machine Learning Algorithms:

Continued advancements in machine learning techniques, including deep learning and reinforcement learning, will enable AI systems to solve more complex and nuanced problems.

AI in Healthcare:

AI will play an increasingly significant role in healthcare, from improving diagnostics and personalized treatment plans to drug discovery and telemedicine.

Autonomous Systems:

Autonomous vehicles, drones, and robots will become more prevalent, transforming industries like transportation, delivery services, and manufacturing.

Natural Language Processing (NLP):

NLP models will become more sophisticated, enabling AI systems to understand and generate human language more accurately. This will lead to improved chatbots, virtual assistants, and language translation services.

AI in Education:

AI-driven personalized education will become more common, catering to individual learning styles and helping students at all levels achieve better outcomes.

Quantum Computing and AI:

The intersection of quantum computing and AI is expected to usher in a new era of computation, solving problems that are currently infeasible for classical computers.

AI Ethics and Regulation:

As AI becomes more integrated into society, there will be an increased focus on ethics, transparency, and regulation to ensure AI systems are developed and used responsibly.

AI Augmentation:

AI will augment human capabilities in various professions, such as healthcare, law, finance, and creative fields, by automating routine tasks and providing data-driven insights.

AI and Cybersecurity:

AI will be crucial for identifying and mitigating cybersecurity threats, as well as protecting critical infrastructure and sensitive data.

AI in Space Exploration:

AI will be used for autonomous navigation, decision-making, and data analysis in space missions, paving the way for more ambitious exploration of the cosmos.

Human-AI Collaboration:

The future will see increased collaboration between humans and AI, with AI systems acting as partners, advisors, and tools to enhance human productivity and creativity.

AI for Mental Health:

AI-driven mental health applications will help with early detection, monitoring, and treatment of mental health conditions.

AI in Art and Entertainment:

AI-generated art, music, and content will continue to evolve, challenging our perceptions of creativity and artistry.

Global AI Collaboration:

International cooperation and knowledge sharing will be crucial for advancing AI research, addressing global challenges, and ensuring responsible AI development.

While the future of AI is promising, it also comes with ethical, societal, and regulatory challenges. Balancing technological advancement with ethical considerations and ensuring equitable access to AI benefits will be key priorities in shaping the future of AI. Additionally, addressing issues related to bias, privacy, and security will be essential for building trust in AI systems.

CHAPTER 10: GETTING STARTED WITH AI

Introduction to Getting Started with AI

Earning money with AI can be achieved through various avenues, whether you're looking to start a business, freelance, or enhance your career within an existing organization. Here are some ways to earn money with AI:

AI Consulting and Services:

Offer AI consulting services to businesses that want to implement AI solutions. This may involve helping them identify AI opportunities, developing AI strategies, or building custom AI applications.

Freelance AI Projects:

Join freelancing platforms like Upwork, Freelancer, or Toptal to find AI-related projects. You can work on tasks ranging from data analysis to developing machine learning models for clients.

Create AI Products:

Develop AI-powered software or applications that solve specific problems or cater to a niche market. You can monetize these products through sales or subscriptions.

AI Training and Education:

Share your AI knowledge and expertise by creating online courses, tutorials, or writing AI-related books. Platforms like Udemy and Coursera allow you to sell your courses.

AI Research and Development:

Work as a researcher or developer in AI-related positions within research institutions, universities, or companies. These roles often offer competitive salaries.

AI Startups:

If you have a unique AI idea or innovation, consider starting an AI-focused startup. Seek funding from investors or venture capitalists to scale your business.

AI Data Labeling Services:

Offer data labeling services for AI training datasets. Many AI projects require accurately labeled data, and you can earn money by providing this service.

AI for Content Creation:

Develop AI tools or platforms that create content, such as automated article generation or content summarization, and offer these services to content creators

AI in Healthcare:

Specialize in AI applications for healthcare, such as medical image analysis or predictive analytics, and offer your services to healthcare providers.

AI in Finance:

Apply AI to financial analysis, algorithmic trading, or risk assessment and provide services to financial institutions.

AI in Marketing:

Use AI for marketing optimization, such as customer segmentation, personalization, and recommendation systems, and offer marketing services to businesses.

AI in E-commerce:
Develop AI-driven recommendation engines and analytics tools for e-commerce platforms to help improve sales and customer satisfaction.

AI in Customer Support:
Create chatbots and virtual assistants that can be integrated into customer support systems to automate responses and improve user experiences.

AI in Legal and Compliance:
Develop AI solutions for legal research, contract analysis, and compliance monitoring, and provide services to legal and regulatory organizations.

AI in Agriculture:
Offer AI-based solutions for precision agriculture, crop monitoring, and yield prediction to farmers and agricultural companies.

AI in Entertainment and Gaming:

Use AI to create interactive experiences, character animation, and content generation for the entertainment and gaming industries.

Remember that success in the AI field often requires continuous learning and staying up-to-date with the latest developments. Building a strong portfolio of projects and establishing a reputation for expertise in a particular AI niche can also help you attract clients and opportunities to earn money with AI.

CONCLUSION

In conclusion, artificial intelligence (AI) is a rapidly evolving field with the potential to revolutionize various industries and aspects of our lives. Whether you're interested in learning AI for personal enrichment, career advancement, or entrepreneurship, there are abundant opportunities to explore and contribute to this exciting domain.

To get started with AI, begin by understanding its fundamentals, including machine learning and deep learning, and then dive into programming and mathematics. Take advantage of online courses, tutorials, books, and practical projects to build your skills. Networking within AI communities and staying informed about research are crucial for staying up-to-date.

Earning money with AI is possible through consulting, freelancing, creating products, offering services, or working in AI-related roles within organizations. The key is to identify your strengths and interests within the AI landscape and leverage them to provide value to clients, employers, or your own ventures.

Remember that AI ethics, responsible development, and staying adaptable in a rapidly changing field are essential considerations as you embark on your AI journey. Embrace a mindset of continuous learning and curiosity, and you'll be well-prepared to thrive in the ever-evolving world of AI.

Written By

Kashan Ajmeri

MASTERING ARTIFICIAL INTELLIGENCE A COMPREHENSIVE GUIDE TO AI TECHNOLOGY

10 CHAPTERS

LIMITED
★ ★ ★ ★ ★
EDITION

www.ingramcontent.com/pod-product-compliance
Lightning Source LLC
Chambersburg PA
CBHW062257290526
45794CB00006B/2592